to Jill Murphy

Copyright © 1989 by Naomi Russell

All rights reserved.

First published in the United States in 1989
by E. P. Dutton, New York, N.Y.,
a division of NAL Penguin Inc.

Originally published in Great Britain in 1989
by Methuen Children's Books,
a division of the Octopus Group Limited,
Michelin House, 81 Fulham Road,
London SW3 6RB

Printed in Singapore by Tien Wah Press
ISBN: 0-525-44468-8
First American Edition   10 9 8 7 6 5 4 3 2 1

The Tree

NAOMI RUSSELL

E. P. DUTTON · NEW YORK

One fall day, a squirrel found
some acorns and piled them up.
He left one behind.

All through the winter,
the acorn lay beneath
the snow.

In the spring, a small
green shoot appeared.

The deer didn't eat it.
The bear didn't step on it.

Slowly it became
a tree, taller

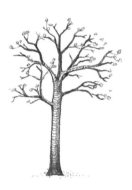

↑ Open

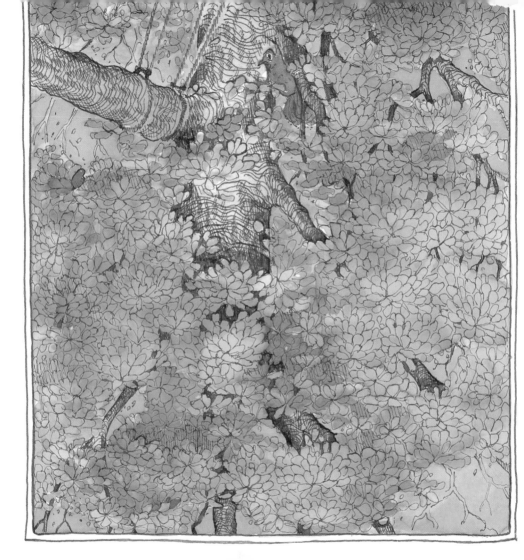

and taller.

As time passed, life went on
around the tree.

Its branches grew wide,
and its trunk grew thick.
Some animals lived in the tree,

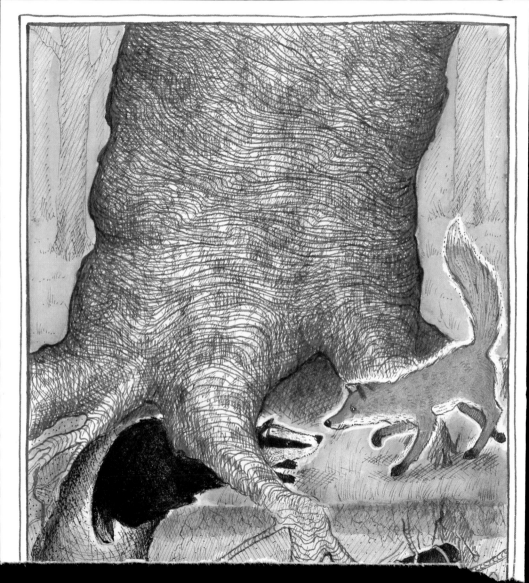

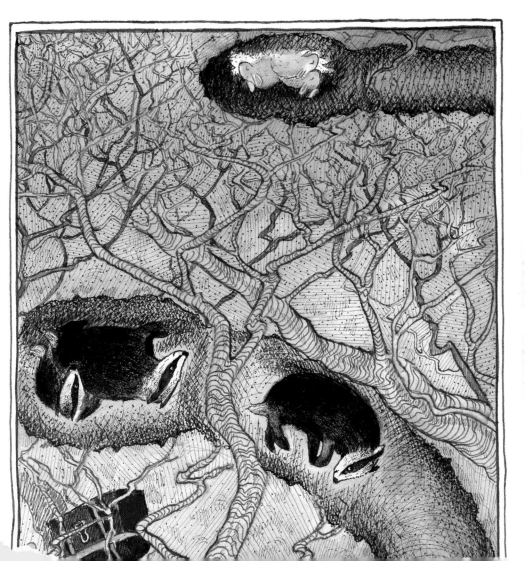

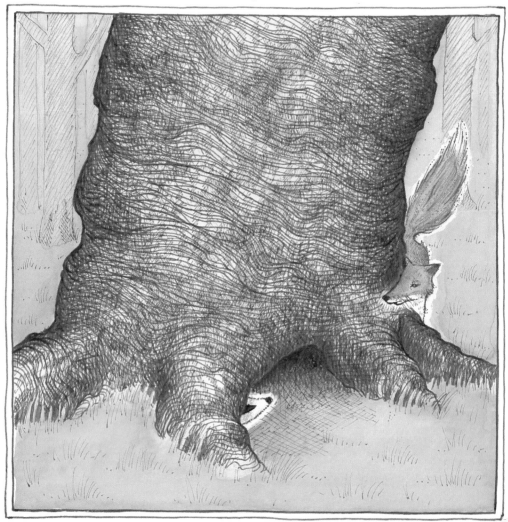

and some lived under it.

Many more years went by.
Now the tree was very old.

A woodcutter chopped it

and down it came.

There were lots of logs
to carry home. Some of
them were made into toys,

and some of them
made a warm fire.

What do you think
was left behind?